Dear D —

I believe we are [owed]
some royalties for these.
While Dino and Jack aren't
actually listed as contributors,
I have no doubt that they
participated in a number of the
following statements:

Jack assisted with Skipper
and Sigourney's statements. Dino
was definitely the ghost writer for
Pinot's poem and I think you'll
find Mary Magdalene's statement
explains a lot.

Finally, I am sure that Dino
[an]d Jack will both be claimants
[in] Fate's suit against Acme Pet
[Pr]oducts and Muddy Waters and Baki's
[co]nversation should be titled
[D]ino and Jack — Enjoy!   Love,
                                    J

DOG

STORIES

Photographs by Jon Weber & Text by Dylan Schaffer

CHRONICLE BOOKS

SAN FRANCISCO

Printed in Singapore.

Library of Congress Cataloging-in-Publication Data:

Weber, Jon.
    Dog stories / photographs by Jon Weber ; text by Dylan Schaffer.
       p. cm.
    ISBN 0-8118-1791-1
    1. Dogs—Pictorial works. 2. Dogs—Fiction. I. Schaffer, Dylan. II. Title.
    SF430.W43 1997
    636.7—dc21   97-8885
                    CIP

Book and cover design: Jon Weber
Composition: Jon Weber
Photographic Printing: Kirk Sanchez
Background Photography: David Campbell
The principal typefaces set in this book are Baskerville MT and Baskerville Expert MT

A special thanks to the San Francisco Society for the Prevention of Cruelty to Animals for the use of their facilities and their continued good work. Chronicle Books has donated a portion of the proceeds of this book to the San Francisco SPCA.

Distributed in Canada by Raincoast Books,
8680 Cambie Street
Vancouver, B.C. V6P 6M9

10 9 8 7 6 5 4 3 2 1

Chronicle Books
85 Second Street
San Francisco, CA 94105

Web Site: www.chronbooks.com

In my dream, Jon and I are sitting on a small green couch in a cage just big enough to take a step in any direction and to reach up and push our fingers through the ceiling of wire mesh. Our cage, and two others like it, are installed in a tiled room that might have been a high school bathroom, its fixtures removed. The glare of fluorescent lights forces us to keep our eyes aimed low. There are some old *Newsweek*s and a radio, but not much else by way of amusement. The sound of a Frisbee spinning on my index finger is interrupted by the creaking of a large metal door.

Abruptly we are beset by a family of stunning golden retrievers—two parents and three unruly pups. Mom and Dad stand virtually motionless in front of the cage, staring at us with a mixture of curiosity and pity. The kids run back and forth, their barks echoing endlessly in the small room. They are possessed of some wild, inexplicable excitement. The parents focus on a large index card pinned to our cage:

These thirty-something friends hope to find a home with space to run and time to pursue their hobbies. Jon likes the water, and Dylan has always wanted to play piano. They are both very well trained and in good physical condition, though Dylan has some lower back problems. Their previous owner had to take a job overseas.

The father looks skeptically at Jon and me and moves on to another cage. Overcome by a mixture of indignation and dejection, I rise. "Listen fella—you could do a lot worse than us. Let me tell you." The pups' yapping cuts off, and the five retrievers, slowly, gingerly, close in on our cage. Their noses press into the steel wire that separates us. As they strain to grasp my meaning, a blush of perplexity and frustration fills their faces. For a moment, the breach between us is filled by a shared longing to understand.

Our relationship with dogs is unique. They wander throughout our homes with impunity. They entertain our children and protect our valuables and give us succor. They share our triumphs and despair. Their loyalty, even in the face of cruelty, is relentless. Their dependence is a gift—of faith and trust. Sometimes, though, we have trouble *hearing* them.

Because dogs seem always to have occupied the same place in our lives, we tend to see them as little more than the effects of their caretakers. The dogs *we* know are sentient, possessing personalities and passions and longings separate from their owners. Theirs is a sharp wit, a profound sense of fairness, a grand passion. They are philosophers and critics and comedians and poets. They are our watchful companions, beacons of civility in a brusque world. And if there has been a gap of understanding between dogs and people, perhaps that is because we have failed to listen, closely.

A STATEMENT BY

Clever

Six days a week I'm man's best friend. I sit and roll over with the best. The postman approaches in horror, the kids work me until I'm ready to drop. I've even been known to fetch a slipper now and again. Don't take me wrong—I'm not complaining—I'm a dog, and that's all there is to it. But Sundays are mine, and if you so much as look at me the wrong way, I'll chew your fingers down to the knuckle.

A STATEMENT BY

Schotze

I'm waiting for you here, bored and cold, while you eat. The street sounds are always the same, and I drift in and out of sleep. Then, dreaming, I'm up at the counter. I turn around to see you outside, face pressed against the window, jostled by diners coming and going. My slightest guilty feeling is overwhelmed by the smell of a bacon-cheeseburger, large order of spicy fries, and chocolate milkshake. Waking up can be such a drag.

Jules

This isn't the life we'd hoped for—protecting people for whom we are no more than living alarm systems, guarding possessions that have no meaning to us. As pups we'd escape into the woods, pretending to be the hunting dogs of kings or the playmates of wild children. But our father was a watchdog, as was his father, and there was never any doubt about our destiny. We have learned to fear strangers, to threaten the unfamiliar, to live on the discomfiting edge of attack. We are hateful because it is useful to others. It is shame, not malice, that causes us to avert our eyes as you approach. One day our strength will wane, and once again we'll be left to the repose of our imaginations.

A DIALOGUE BETWEEN

Merlin & Palermo

M: *What makes us dogs?*

P: *Why do you ask?*

M: *I sometimes think the things that make me easily identifiable as a dog—my bark, my smell—are the least important things about me, about us. We are unique among the species, but for reasons seldom articulated.*

P: *That is because we live in a borrowed world. Like all domesticated creatures we exist as a subset of the experiences of our masters. And like all slaves we are valued exclusively for those traits which make us useful: we are obedient, we are protective. But our trials, loves, hopes, and dreams, these are obscured by our owners' need for us to be dog-like.*

M: *So what is the one thing that most makes you a dog?*

P: *I can serve without being servile. And you?*

M: *I can see into the hearts of those who love me.*

Bogart

You are under the erroneous impression that each time you pick up a slimy old tennis ball or bacteria-ridden stick and wave it around like a mad person, I experience some kind of giant mood improvement. Believe me, I'd rather relax on the couch in the air-conditioned living room than spend hours in the heat, chasing after foul-tasting toys, back and forth, until you lose interest. Whether it pleases me or not, I am driven by my genes, coerced even, to retrieve, to bury, to hunt. The cat does not appear to be similarly burdened. I've seen him sit for hours in the cool of the hallway closet, unapologetically cleaning himself. Your opinion of him does not rise and fall with each day's test of speed or endurance. I view his nonchalance with a perturbing blend of envy and resentment. And I question whether you would expose him *to such a panoply of disease-laden playthings.*

A LETTER BY

Orbit

To the Editor:

I read with mounting frustration your recent column on the subject of canine hairstyling [William Halberstrom, "Poodle Aplomb"]. In Mr. Halberstrom's uncommonly ignorant view, a poodle's distinctive cut is a contrivance of the idol rich: having tired of redecorating their houses and children, the upper classes thrill to fleecing and coifing their trusted companions.

FYI: The word "poodle" is probably derived from the German *Pudelhund* (loosely, "splashing-dog"), which refers to our love of water. For centuries we have numbered among the treasured hunting dogs, specializing in the retrieval of waterfowl. The styling niceties that are so amusing to Mr. Halberstrom in fact were developed to increase our effectiveness in the hunt: shaved limbs offer swiftness in water; hair is left on the rear legs to protect the ankles from rheumatism; the pompom on the tail (which your reporter likened to a manicured bush) permits an owner to track her dog in the water during retrieval of an angry and often dangerous bird.

Mr. Halberstrom appears to have been too busy taking tea with his subjects' owners to discover the *facts* relevant to his article.

Sincerely,

Orbit

A STATEMENT BY

Coco

I live for this moment. After the approach and flight, quite honestly, the water is a bit of a let down. Think back to your first kiss. At some point you knew it was going to happen, and soon you'd never be the same. The electricity and confusion of the moment takes over. Every second is as happily painful as it is eternal. I get that feeling every time. The leash comes off and in a flash I know no one can stop me. I pause, and then fly to the edge without thought of past or future. I would trade every bone I've ever had to live forever in the instant before descent.

A STATEMENT BY
Gudzi

Proud to say I've lived my entire life on the fifteenth floor of the noble prewar you see in the distance. Time was, a word like "decorum" had teeth—none of this unapologetic butt sniffing you see without trying these days; a dog understood his position. Last week a rock-and-roll man and his three shrill chihuahuas took over the fifth floor. New money, I say. Next thing you know I'll be obliged to hobnob with half-breeds, or worse.

A STATEMENT BY

Skipper

I recommend the following strategy in choosing an owner, which may otherwise prove a disappointing endeavor. While a master with a gentle disposition is preferable, beware of unrestrained sentiment, which can be a sign of emotional instability. Close attention to physical condition is imperative: check teeth, tongue, body fat, and so on. Choose an overseer with excellent health, but without exceptional speed or strength. For maximum autonomy, she should not be able to catch or restrain you. What kind of living space and yard does your suitor have to offer? Look before you leap. If you are a busy dog, you may prefer a pretrained owner. Has she been taught to feed, walk, and throw a ball? Does she respond to your commands? One effective tactic is to disgorge your most recent meal immediately upon greeting a potential owner. This is an excellent test of a human being's genuine temperament.

A POEM BY

Pinot

I'm told that my conduct is draining,
Despite the vast sums gone to training.
But to heel or to sit?
For a dog of my wit?
To me—poetry's more entertaining.

So I spend my days dreaming up verses,
In spite of occasional curses
From my owner, who claims,
That I'm hardly house-trained
Causing headaches she so often nurses.

I say it's simply not fair
To measure, contrast or compare
Myself to the kitty,
Who though properly pretty,
Hasn't a tenth of my flair.

In the end I'm sure you'll agree,
That a dog of such genius as me,
Must nurture defiance,
Not boring compliance,
To sustain creativity.

A STATEMENT BY

Brutus

What are you lookin' at?

A STATEMENT BY

Walker

Okay, so why four *clocks in the kitchen? A timer on the microwave, another on the stove, a digital clock on the radio (which you might turn down while I'm eating), and the analogue Mickey Mouse hanging precariously over the breakfast table. Do they account for your days? I gotta tell you I'm beginning to feel a tad superior, free as I am from your time obsession, rarely late, and happily oblivious to my own mortality.*

A STATEMENT BY

Lane

When I was a pup, it took very little to propel me into a frenzy of enthusiasm. The sound of the front door opening or your heavy footsteps coming down the stairs sent me bouncing off walls. Your inadvertent elbow touched my leash, and I was off into a delirium of tail-wagging. And while sometimes I was baffled by your attempts to train me, you'd never have accused me of indifference. Time takes its toll, though. It's not so much that you can't teach an old dog new tricks. Rather, with age, it simply takes more to inspire us.

Sixer

That stale August afternoon I watched from the porch as the tall man got out of his car—shaking badly. Instinctively, he checked the front bumper, surprised to find nothing. A crowd had gathered quickly, so it took him a moment to find the dog. I had known Carly, though not well. The driver looked down at the stricken animal, muttering to no one: "She jumped out, I didn't see her." The dog appeared unhurt, but could only lift her head. She knew, as I did, that the damage was serious and irreversible. Soon her owner would arrive, followed by a final trip to the vet.

Carly's eyes told a hundred stories, of travels, of friends and rivals, of secret loves. She laughed at her recklessness and cursed the cold she now felt stretching through her once sturdy frame. Perhaps I should have gone to her. But I sat, motionless, savoring the sweet summer heat, waiting for the smell of mourning.

A STATEMENT BY

Jessie

Walking by your colossal image on the billboard ("Get Met, It Pays"), my mind reels and I find myself deconstructing Snoopy. We all wanted to be Joe Cool—jazz-cat sunglasses, strut-dog boogie, driving indifferently by Lassie in our wing-tipped Cadillac convertible, slung low in the seats, heads bobbing to a Vince Guaraldi beat bass. The sophisticated canine, the James Bond of Beagles. Old man Schultz knew the score: you were just bad enough, just smart enough, just Zen enough to hold the whole show together. If we could have climbed inside the TV, the magic box, we would have strapped ourselves behind you in the Sopwith Camel to battle the Red Baron. Did you hear our roar when you laid a wet one on Lucy? You—the lawyer, the novelist, the philosopher—you helped us see the possibilities.

And though now we find you selling insurance, our electric memories are not muted. We grew up together and so we are relieved—you turn out to be one of us after all.

A STATEMENT BY

Jolie Blond

Must I receive the blame for every otherwise unattributable household offense—the inexplicably missing sock, the unwitnessed stain, the unguarded pork chop, vanished? Without a legion of trouble-making assistants, I simply cannot have been responsible for visiting so much havoc on this estimable dwelling. I admit only to the following:

The sticky spot on the entryway carpet, which no doubt has marred the reputation of this family among its many highly placed visitors, is, as suspected, the remains of young Joshua's birthday cake. And yes, Jennifer's Hollywood Barbie did sacrifice her head at the alter of my chewing-lust. The remnants may be retrieved (might I suggest a closed casket) underneath the living room couch. Finally, the fact that you returned from your vacation to find Mittens stranded in the tree was indeed the result of my having stalked her for the preceding twelve hours. To describe the long-standing provocation that led to this conflict would only result in renewed rancor, and I, for one, am in favor of detente.

Sigourney

To you it is just a walk, twenty absentminded minutes between waking and coffee. But to me it is a paradigm for our complex alliance—an elaborate dance of manners. I sit, static, paralyzed by anticipation, except for my tail, which slaps the floor, left then right. Squeezing through the front door, I taste the cold air. I feel the stern snap of the leash on my collar, and a shiver sails through me. At first I tarry over minutia—an oil stain, a gum wrapper. Just as your patience ebbs I amble past you, taking the helm. Digging my legs into the pavement, I point my nose into the wind, hauling you through space and time. I see if you're awake by feigning interest in a dead pigeon—like clockwork, your resistance comforts me. Neither looking at each other nor daring to separate, we are like old lovers.

A STATEMENT BY

Shayla

In the old days I worked the narco beat at LAX—
cheerless work. Little girls with bricks of heroin
strapped beneath their party dresses, old men praying
the balloons in their bellies would hold for a few more
hours, terrified of dying far from home. I'm not ashamed
to say I let a few walk right by me in my eight years,
especially the ones who looked like they might be in it
to keep food on the table in some village in Colombia
or Nigeria. I smile when I remember the cops admiring
my nose. Frankly, I never had much of a scent for
drugs, but the smell of fear, that you never miss.

Muddy Waters & Baki

MW: *When I die, I want to remembered for something significant— something profound.*

B: *I'm on the verge of figuring out how to open the meat freezer in the basement, and you're pestering me with this existential nonsense.*

MW: *I think we need to develop a new approach to the mailman.*

B: *What is it with you? Running and slamming into the front door while growling and bearing our fangs has worked in the past, and I see no need to abandon that approach now.*

MW: *How about this: when he opens the door, we raise our heads just enough to let him know we're awake, but we do nothing.*

B: *You've lost your mind.*

MW: *He'll think we've lost interest, he'll be totally off his guard, perilously complacent. Then in a few days, he'll look through the window, but we'll be on the stairs where he can't see us. He cracks open the door, we wait. He takes a step inside, we wait. As he leans over to the mailbox, and not a moment sooner, we let go our best hounds of hell imitation.*

B: *You are a visionary.*

A STATEMENT BY

Patsy Cline

They sold off the last of the litter today. For the days they were with me I held my breath because they were blind and feeble and demanding. I fed them dutifully and offered them protection from the night chill. But long ago I banished any thought that they could, or even should, stay, so I remained aloof, uncommitted. Perhaps they tasted detachment on my breast, or smelled indifference creeping from beneath my coat.

I can exhale now, but I am left empty. Will I recognize my sons and daughters if they return? How many times will I come to this place, to stare down the long road that stole them from me?

A STATEMENT BY

Mookie

I find it disturbing that you use the word "dog" to describe an unfaithful man. Just yesterday I overheard a young woman in the park lamenting her boyfriend's tendency to stray, to which her companion replied: "He's a dog; he'll never change."

You mistakenly assume that we bring to mating the emotional and aesthetic complexities of your more "evolved" species. By likening this particularly distasteful human behavior to that of a dog, there is a tendency to see it as driven by instinct, and therefore to excuse it. I don't deny there are ways in which we are alike. But in calling your adulterers "dogs," you demean our entirely blameless and genetically beneficial inclination to procreate across breeds and among a variety of partners.

A STATEMENT BY

Scout

Am I behind the fence, or are you?

A STATEMENT BY

Ella

Does it trouble you to learn that our behavior in your presence is a put-on? We understand what you expect and we conduct ourselves accordingly. Indeed, we are great believers in fidelity to the given social order. To reject such an arrangement in our own relations would be to invite chaos. So, you play the generous master, and we take the role of the adoring servant. No matter what exceptional deeds we've accomplished in your absence, when you arrive we scurry to your feet, filling the room with delighted, even witless, abandon.

And though our relations are a drama we partake in without complaint, they are theater nonetheless. At the end of the evening the audience files out, makeup is removed, costumes are safely stored. And the actors, adrenaline ebbing, catch each others' glances and acknowledge, silently, that the play offers quite a comfort in this savage world.

A STATEMENT BY

Ladee

You are the wounded, the stricken, the bloody. I am the hunter. You are the fugitive, the convicted, the damned. I am the law. You are the tempted, the sinner, the wicked. I am the devil. You are the guilty, the fallen, the shamed. I am the conscience. You are the fire's light. I am the rain. You are life, and I am death. I am the hound.

A STATEMENT BY

Indie

I'll grant, there is an ounce of authenticity in the dejected expression on my face each morning as you prepare to leave. You know the look: tail wagging furiously, eyes wide and slightly misty, ears up, as if to say, "Are you absolutely certain you intend to leave me here? Perhaps this is all some kind of silly misunderstanding." I wait for the sad trio of sounds: the door shutting behind you, the key in the lock, the engine of your old car, after a few tries, turning over.

But invariably the gloom swiftly lifts. I march over to the living room window to make sure you haven't parked on a side street and returned to spy. Just then it hits me: freedom, sweet freedom! The unguarded pantry, a glut of socks, a deluge of savory garbage. And the cats, asleep upstairs, unsuspecting. Sometimes I lie on the couch all day, genuinely paralyzed by the magnitude of my prerogative.

Fred

Let me put this into perspective for you. You're walking down the street, minding your own business. You do not see ominous clouds in the distance. You do not hear foreboding music. Without warning, the swollen feet of a thirty-foot, bald monster appear before you. The ghoul is mumbling incomprehensibly and apparently wants to kill you because it has directed its hideous hands at your neck. Your inability to speak the creature's language prevents any kind of bargaining. Although the beast stinks intensely, you hesitate to step back and risk angering him. His intentions are unfathomable, but you expect to die at any moment. Without warning, the monster kneels down, his rotten breath and Brillo-covered face now inches from your own. His hand reaches in and . . .

Next time, think before you stick your hand in the face of an unfamiliar dog.

A STATEMENT BY

Max

You must be one of them artistes, huh? Hey, I'm with you, I'm with you—I spent two years with a traveling circus as Maximilian, the Mongrel Minstrel. I killed 'em. That was before Tom—that's him behind me. He's strictly backyards and barbecues, if you know what I mean. The guy's a peach and all, but sometimes I miss the life. Hey, how about you and I blow this scene and grab a drink someplace?

A STATEMENT BY

Bear

What made me eat the whole tube of latex paint I can't begin to explain. Sometimes you eat it just because it's there, calling out to you. It wasn't all that bad going down, really. And whatever slight gastric disturbance resulted, the look on your face when you saw my green tongue was well worth it.

A STATEMENT BY

Molly

Are you the one? Me: attractive, slim, shortish, luxuriously hirsute, ready for commitment and puppies. You: five-something canine, long hair, natural fiber leashes; you'd hold it past three fire hydrants to reach the eucalyptus in the soft sand by the waves every time. Can you handle that I'm better trained than you? Picture and letter appreciated.

A STATEMENT BY

Mary Magdalene

It has often been suggested that each year in a dog's life is worth seven human years. But surprisingly little thought has been given to the implications of this notion. Think about it: one to seven. No wonder we seem a bit high-strung. While you fritter away your days, we're busy trying to live at seven times the pace. Our meals ought to be seven times the size of yours. If we chase cars, maybe we're just trying to catch a ride? Have you ever stopped to consider how long it would take you to walk everywhere? If we get a little carried away when you come home after work, can you blame us? Your watch says you've been gone for eight hours, but to us its been two and a half days. Believe me, we don't relish the idea of waking you at 5:00 a.m. It's just that we're in kind of a rush.

A STATEMENT BY

Jones

Our unique intimacy has, in my opinion, resulted in an appalling deterioration of manners. When "nature" calls, the following rules should be strictly observed. KEEP YOUR DISTANCE! We do not appreciate crowding! KEEP IT TO YOURSELF! When the law requires you to clean up after us, I see no need for comments of any kind. No one is listening anyway. KEEP IT DOWN! If you're with a friend, and you must continue your conversation, please speak softly—this is a delicate affair. WHAT'S YOUR RUSH? Do we knock on the bathroom door while you are indisposed? You may want to carry reading material. PLASTIC NOT PAPER! When it comes to "collection," for obvious reasons, I urge you to set aside environmental concerns. STAY ON THE GRASS! Take the extra five minutes to find a patch of lawn. The sidewalk is rough, hard, and cold. IT'S NONE OF YOUR BEESWAX! You needn't stare—you'll know we're through when you feel a tug on the leash.

A POEM BY

Bella

You accuse me of reeking, of rotting, of stinking,
As though I had done something wrong.
And to my horror, you say with a glower,
"The time between baths is too long."

Unplug the tub and bury your scrub brush,
Sit down, I'll try to explain
The critical nature of odors you think
Are simply too vile to sustain.

You rise in the morning a bit of a wreck,
And then to the bathroom retreat,
To apply lotions and perfumes and potions
From your crown to the tips of your feet.

And though time-consuming, and no doubt quite costly,
You douse yourself hoping to seize
A suitable mate with appropriate traits,
He or she whom your fragrance might please.

We mutts are no different, our image is vital,
Our smells give important details.
I carefully cultivate scents to attract
A whole host of available males.

So quit your complaining and buy yourself noseplugs,
Lysol or Glade by the crate,
I'll cling to my bouquet, no matter what you say,
The bath simply will have to wait.

Sam

One hundred years after the birth of Christ, the popular view held that rabies was caused by worms. An obscure Roman agriculturist named Columella found a dog who had been in a vicious fight. The dog's tail had been bitten off, and Columella observed what he believed were the rabies-causing parasites. In fact what he saw were the dog's tendons, its tangled flesh. In a rush to gain credit for his discovery, wrong as it was, Columella advocated the removal of dogs' tails to guard against infection.

When I look over my shoulder and see my sad stump, there is always a moment of grief. Not for myself—I've long accepted my disfigurement—but for the bewildering ignorance of your species.

Jake

To the Chairperson, Acme Pet Products:

Enclosed please find one Acme "Magi-Collar," which I am returning for a full refund ($29.99). This item was purchased by Mrs. Agnes E. Smith; immediate reimbursement should be made to her.

I do not fault you or your worthy firm for conception of the Magi-Collar, which I will assume is the brainchild of a sadist who has secreted him or herself in your midst. Still, it is my duty to bring your attention to the following: your costly product contains a large number of pointy metal spikes that, when the collar is attached to a leash, issue painfully into the neck of the wearer. Mrs. Smith, for the most part a gentle and cooperative owner, has taken to employing the Magi-Collar to thwart a variety of conduct never before deemed offensive (e.g., cat chasing, garbage rummaging, and such). We have not resorted to such unpleasantness in the past, and I daresay I'm too old to begin to endure such assaults.

I trust your torturous product will prosper in these days of indecency. There was a time, Mr. Chairman, perhaps a better time, when relations between our species were conducted with greater civility.

Sincerely,

Jake

A HAIKU BY

Ben

Safe outside steel fence
you say horns of dilemma;
inside they're just horns.

A STATEMENT BY

Duke

Like any extraordinary ability, my sense of smell (perhaps ten million times finer than your own) is often a great burden. I sense not only the blood of the wounded fox but also the dread and grieving of the animals who look on as she falters. While my nose tracks the escaped prisoner, I cannot avoid the essence of the family he has left behind, or of his victims' fetid desire for revenge. While I lead a search party, bravely laboring to find travelers lost in a storm, I recognize the odor of death advancing. And though we both know the scent of your lover's perfume while she waits behind the front door, only I can smell her disquiet as she prepares to leave you.

A STATEMENT BY

Blackie

As fond as we become of one another, there is,
I believe, an essential and insurmountable gap
between us. You think we chew up your Luis
Vuitton briefcase because you cut short our walk.
You think we sit because you reward us or scold
us, or even beat us, when we do not sit. You
think we are pleased when you arrive because
you are the alpha and we are the beta. You think
we growl at strangers because they remind us of
our former owners who mistreated us. You have
projected yourselves onto us, and while ultimately
harmless, this leaves you puzzled or frustrated
or disillusioned when we fail to conform to your
expectations. We do what we do, no more and
no less, because it is our nature.

*For Sophie, Pam, and Nancy, who held the net while
I did my high-wire act.* —DS

*For the Kitty, who taught me to love; for the Owl,
who taught me to see; for the Buddha, who taught me
perfection; and for the Dogs, who loved me.* —JW